Today's Superst★rs

Entertainment

Jackie Chan

by Amy Stone

GARETH STEVENS
GS
PUBLISHING

A Member of the WRC Media Family of Companies

Please visit our web site at: www.garethstevens.com
For a free color catalog describing Gareth Stevens Publishing's
list of high-quality books and multimedia programs, call
1-800-542-2595 (USA) or 1-800-387-3178 (Canada).
Gareth Stevens Publishing's fax: (414) 332-3567.

Library of Congress Cataloging-in-Publication Data

Stone, Amy, 1947-
  Jackie Chan / by Amy Stone.
    p. cm. — (Today's superstars. Entertainment)
  Includes bibliographical references and index.
  ISBN-13: 978-0-8368-7648-2 (lib. bdg.)
  1. Cheng, Long, 1954- —-Juvenile literature. 2. Motion picture
actors and actresses—China—Biography—Juvenile literature. I. Title.
PN2878.C52S76   2007
791.4302'8092—dc22
  [B]   2006030680

This edition first published in 2007 by
Gareth Stevens Publishing
A Member of the WRC Media Family of Companies
330 West Olive Street, Suite 100
Milwaukee, WI 53212 USA

This edition copyright © 2007 by Gareth Stevens, Inc.

Editor: Gini Holland
Art direction and design: Tammy West
Picture research: Sabrina Crewe

Photo credits: cover © Kirsten Neumann/Reuters/Corbis; p. 5 © Corbis
Sygma; p. 7 Dimension Films/Everett Collection; pp. 9, 11 © Bob Krist/
Corbis; pp. 10, 19, 20, 21 Everett Collection; p. 13 © Bettmann/Corbis;
p. 15 © Wen Huang/China Features/Corbis Sygma; p. 16 Associated Press;
p. 25 © Miramax/courtesy Everett Collection; p. 27 © Columbia TriStar
Television/courtesy Everett Collection; p. 28 © Frank Trapper/Corbis

Printed in the United States of America

1 2 3 4 5 6 7 8 9 10 10 09 08 07 06

Contents

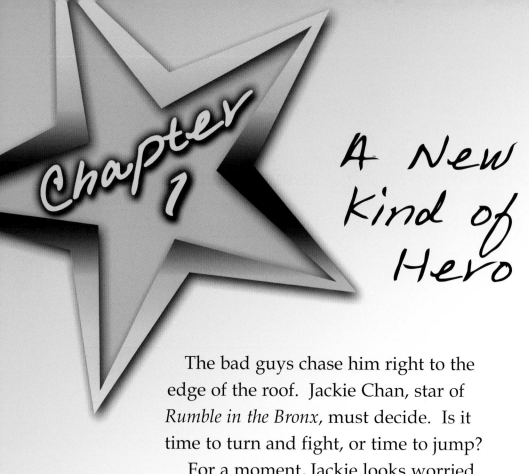

Chapter 1

A New Kind of Hero

The bad guys chase him right to the edge of the roof. Jackie Chan, star of *Rumble in the Bronx*, must decide. Is it time to turn and fight, or time to jump?

For a moment, Jackie looks worried. Then he bursts into a run and leaps — off the top of the parking structure. He soars! Then he drops and drops some more. He lands on the balcony of a nearby building. Grabbing his ankle, Jackie moans with pain. Many motion-picture action heroes make their stunts look easy. Jackie makes them look real. Jackie plays a hero, but a very human one.

When Jackie Chan fights, he sweats and he grunts. Sometimes he cowers in fear. "Audiences want to see someone who's

Risky Business

Jackie's movie stunts don't always work out. One nearly killed him. During the filming of *Armour of God* (1986), Jackie jumped off a castle wall. He planned to grab a tree branch to soften his fall. Somehow, he missed it. When he hit the rocky ground, he cracked his skull. A piece of it lodged in his brain. Doctors saved his life, but Jackie still has a hole in his head. A plastic plug keeps it closed.

Critics did not love Jackie's film *Armour of God*, but they did like his stunts. Not only did Jackie climb to dangerous heights, he fell onto a hot-air balloon.

just a man," Jackie says. He must be right. Jackie Chan is one of the most admired action heroes of all time. He has starred in dozens of films.

Fans the world over flock to Jackie's movies. They love seeing him perform. A highly skilled martial artist, Jackie uses several styles to fight his enemies. In the end, he always wins. Along the way, however, he isn't afraid to make a fool of himself. At first, he loses the girl and a fight or two. Audiences feel sympathy for Jackie. They love the man as much as the action.

Getting into Mischief
Jackie's first highly successful film was *Drunken Master*. Shown in Asia, the movie featured Jackie as the martial arts master, Wong Fei Hung. Wong is also a Chinese folk hero. Many Asian movies had been made about this master. Audiences were used to seeing Wong as a serious man. Jackie, however, showed him as a teenager who kept getting into mischief.

Fact File

Jackie is not afraid to perform action movie stunts. But he is afraid of the doctor's needle. He hates getting shots!

The mischief made audiences laugh. He also showed the master's martial arts' skills. Jackie's fighting skills impressed audiences. Jackie had begun to set himself up as a new kind of action moviemaker who added humor to the plots.

In his films, Jackie leaps, flips, dives, and fights. His skills amaze his fans. He makes it all look so easy. How and when did he learn these many skills? Jackie's story begins a long time ago in Hong Kong.

Jackie manages to hang on when this helicopter from *Supercop* — originally released as *Police Story III* — crashes through billboards.

Fact File

In 2006, Jackie was voted one of Asia's Top 100 "Hunks."

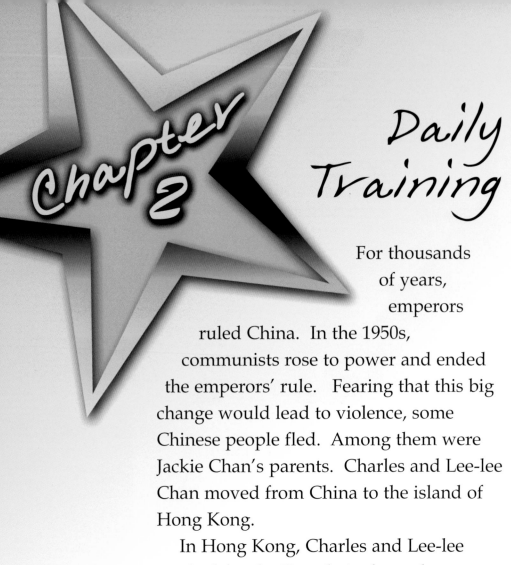

Chapter 2

Daily Training

For thousands of years, emperors ruled China. In the 1950s, communists rose to power and ended the emperors' rule. Fearing that this big change would lead to violence, some Chinese people fled. Among them were Jackie Chan's parents. Charles and Lee-lee Chan moved from China to the island of Hong Kong.

In Hong Kong, Charles and Lee-lee worked for the French Ambassador. Charles cooked and Lee-lee cleaned the ambassador's huge house. The Chans worked hard but made little money. They lived in the back of the house, in two small, windowless rooms.

In 1954, the Chans had a baby boy. They named him Chan Kong-sang. The name means "Chan born in Hong Kong."

(Later, Chan Kong-sang's name changed to Jackie Chan—but that gets ahead of the story!)

Charles Chan wanted his young son to turn into a good and strong man. In Charles' eyes, such a man can put up with, or endure, physical pain. Learning to endure pain takes daily training. When Jackie turned four, Charles began to train him. After yanking his sleepy son out of bed each morning, he led him outside. There, he made him lift large rice bags filled with sand. Each bag was half as tall as Jackie and weighed about 25 pounds (11 kilograms). Charles also taught him the

One of the highest points on the island of Hong Kong is Victoria Peak. As a young child, Jackie lived in a neighborhood that surrounds the peak.

Fact File

Jackie weighed about 12 pounds (5 kilograms) at birth. This is very heavy for a newborn baby. His mother nicknamed him "Pao Pao," meaning "Cannonball."

Rush Hour costarred Jackie and Chris Tucker as detectives. The comic interactions between the two helped make the movie a success.

Fact File

Jackie's father, Charles, cooked very tasty — and sometimes fancy — meals for his family. But Jackie loves simple food best of all. He would rather buy a bowl of rice and pork from a street vendor then dine at a fancy restaurant.

basics of northern style kung fu. When Jackie turned five, his parents sent him to school. They hoped he would do well. He didn't. Jackie hated sitting still. He would fall out of his chair on purpose, just to make his classmates laugh. The Chans pulled their little boy out of school. "What will become of him?" they worried.

How Kung Fu Began

About A.D. 500, a monk from India left his country. He traveled to a temple in China. He hoped to teach some Chinese monks the lessons of a new religion called Buddhism. To help them, he wrote a book of exercises. The exercises required intense mental focus and physical strength. After doing the exercises, the monks often felt calm and peaceful. Buddhists believe that feeling peaceful is important for a person's spirit. The Chinese monks called these exercises kung fu.

Performing kung fu depends on learning the basics. At first, students spend hours simply stretching. Stretching helps build muscle. Later, they learn to jump, kick, and punch.

Chapter 3

Under Pain of Injury

Jackie's life changed in 1961. His father, Charles Chan, accepted an offer for a job in Australia. It paid a lot. But it didn't pay enough to take his wife and son to Australia. "When I leave Hong Kong, who will teach Jackie how to become a man?" Charles wondered. He found Jackie a new teacher, Master Yu Jim-Yuen. Master Yu ran the China Drama Academy for children.

The academy trained girls and boys to perform in the Chinese opera. American opera features singing and acting. Chinese opera adds tumbling, acrobatics, and martial arts. For ten years, Jackie lived at the academy. He trained under Master Yu.

In the 1960s, Master Yu decided that the best of his thirty students should begin performing in public. He picked seven top students. One of them was Jackie. Called the Seven Little Fortunes, the students performed in many operas. They became stars!

Master Yu ran a strict program. He made students sleep on floor mats and train for seventeen hours a day. Master Yu rarely forgave mistakes. A student performing a handstand had to hold the pose for half an hour. If he fell, Master hit him with a cane.

Jackie's mother, Lee-lee Chan, left Hong Kong for Australia in 1963. Nine-year-old Jackie stayed at the China

Jackie liked silent film star and comedian Harold Lloyd. Lloyd's stunts, such as this from *Safety Last* (1923), inspired Jackie. In *Project A*, Jackie hangs from a clock.

Fact File

The China Drama Academy gave all its students new names. When Chan Kong-sang (Jackie) entered the Academy in 1961, he became Yeun Lo. All the students called each other brother and sister.

Drama Academy. Master Yu adopted Jackie as his godson. Jackie hoped for favored treatment. He didn't get it. Master Yu expected more of Jackie than he did of his other students. One day, Master told the students to "freeze." "Hold your legs high in the air for five minutes," he commanded. He ordered Jackie to hold his leg high for ten minutes. "Now that you are my godson," said Master Yu, "you have to set an example for the others."

Practice, Practice, Practice

Day after day, year after year, Jackie practiced. He jumped from high places — without a net. He learned to land without hurting himself. He practiced flips, handstands, handsprings, tumbles, and martial arts moves, over and over. Jackie says he never learned to perform any one move a whole lot better than the other students. He did, however, learn them all. Jackie's small build helped him perform the moves quickly. His mastery and speed

Fact File

Some of the China Drama Academy students hurt themselves badly while training under the Academy Master in the 1960s. At that time, the laws protected the Master against complaints from parents.

14

have served him well in the action-movie business.

Jackie finished his training just before he turned seventeen. Sadly, Jackie and his classmates could not get steady jobs with Chinese opera companies. Chinese opera was no longer popular. Jackie and his friends did not have math or reading skills. They faced problems finding any work at all. Many turned to the growing Hong Kong film industry. Action-movie directors needed stuntmen. Jackie hoped to become one.

Jackie and other students at the China Drama Academy spent up to seventeen hours a day learning martial arts and acrobatics.

Fact File

After his movies end with a list of credits, Jackie often shows his stunt mistakes. Many mistakes have caused the injuries that Jackie is famous for.

How Do They Do It?

To pull off their astonishing acts, stunt men and women need talent and training — and lots of it! In schools around the world, students learn to do death-defying stunts for the movies. They learn hand-to-hand combat. Riding and falling off horses, steering a car during a high-speed chase, and falling from high distances are all part of the training. They even learn how to survive being set on fire.

Stunt performers sometimes suffer injuries. Once in a great while, a stunt person is killed during movie production. Some think that stunts are too dangerous. They say that stunt people should be replaced with special effects. Others insist that computer-made stunts look fake. Maybe the best choice lies in-between. Many of today's films mix computer graphics with human stunt work to great effect.

Jackie's role as a Hong Kong detective in *Supercop* won praise for its fight scenes. Jackie uses a kung-fu kick to flatten his enemy.

No Stunt Too Risky

Jackie Chan has risen to the top in the action-movie business. But he started at the bottom. After leaving the China Drama Academy in 1971, Jackie found a job with the Movie Town studio in Hong Kong. The studio made low-budget, poor-quality martial arts movies. Jackie began as a junior stuntman.

On the set, Jackie admired the senior stuntmen's courage. Jackie says they lived by the *lung fu mo shi*, or the dragon tiger creed. This creed says you should always show you are as powerful as a dragon and as brave as a tiger. When a senior stuntman got hurt during a stunt, he got back up and did it again.

Jackie had plenty of ambition. He wanted to rise from junior stuntman to senior stuntman. To do this, he needed to catch the eye of the stunt coordinator.

Jackie soon saw his chance. One day, a Movie Town studio director ordered a senior stuntman to fall off a 15-foot- (5.6-meter-) high balcony, backward. The director ordered the stunt done without a wire. Stunt performers sometimes wear very thin wires attached to harnesses beneath their shirts. The wires run to pulleys controlled by ropes. If a fall spins out of control, putting a stuntman in danger, the ropes are pulled taut or tight. This action slows and cushions the fall.

The stunt coordinator told the senior stuntman not to do the stunt. He feared the stuntman would end up dead. Jackie, however, figured that if he timed it right, he could do the stunt, land on his feet— and walk away. So he volunteered.

Try Anything
Jackie did the stunt perfectly. He won the respect of the stunt coordinator. He also won a promotion. During the early 1970s, Jackie became known as a stuntman who would try anything. He even performed in

Fact File

The sound tracks of many of Jackie's Hong Kong-made movies feature Jackie as a singer. In Asia, Jackie is a popular music star.

Bruce Lee — The "Mighty Dragon"

Even before his first hit movie, *The Big Boss* (1971), martial artist Bruce Lee had many fans. A Chinese American, Bruce had costarred in the popular TV series, *The Green Hornet*. Fans loved his quick, tough-guy moves. He had learned these moves in Hong Kong in the 1940s and early 1950s. He studied under the famous kung fu master, Yip Men.

In his 1973 block-bluster film *Enter the Dragon*, Bruce shows "the art of the intercepting fist." First, he places his fist about an inch from his enemy's chest. With a lightening-fast thrust of his shoulder, Bruce knocks his enemy down flat.

Bruce died in 1973, just before the much-younger Jackie broke into action movies. People often compared Jackie to Bruce. But Jackie says, "I never wanted to be the next Bruce Lee. I just wanted to be the best Jackie Chan." Jackie says that if it hadn't been for Bruce Lee, Jackie could not have succeeded. Bruce opened fans' eyes to the beauty and excitement of martial arts.

Enter the Dragon made martial artist Bruce Lee (*left*) a superstar. It showcased a fighting style that Lee invented, *Jeet Kune Do*.

Bruce Lee's best-loved Hong-Kong-made film, *Fist of Fury*. He did the stunts for the head villain, Mr. Suzuki. When Bruce kicked Mr. Suzuki through a wall, Jackie's body flew 15 feet (5.6 meters) before hitting the ground.

Stunt work left little time for a personal life. Jackie, however, found time for his very first love — Oh Jang. Jackie had met Oh Jang toward the end of his Academy days, while performing in a Chinese opera. She was an opera actor, too. Oh Jang cared for Jackie, but the two had to meet in secret. Oh Jang's well-to-do father did not approve of Jackie. He saw only a poor young man whose future job prospects did not look very promising. Oh Jang obeyed her father. She ended her relationship with Jackie. She broke Jackie's heart, but Jackie remembers Oh Jang with fondness.

After Oh Jang's opera career ended, she ran a women's dress shop

Fact File

In 1983, Jackie formed the Jackie Chan Stunt Team. The team is made up of martial artists and stuntmen that Jackie has trained and trusts. He will use only these team members to perform the stunts in his movies.

in Hong Kong. When Jackie became rich, he often sent his female employees to the shop. He gave them money to buy lots of dresses so that Oh Jang's business did well.

After Bruce Lee died in 1973, so did interest in action movies. Out of work and money, Jackie moved from Hong Kong to Australia. He lived with his parents. He found a construction job, working for a large man named Jack.

When the other workers asked Jack his assistant's name, Jack thought they would never remember Kong-sang. So he said, "Just call him little Jack." The workers changed "little Jack" to Jackie. From then on, Chan Kong-sang became Jackie Chan. This name stuck.

Jackie performed a number of stunts in Bruce Lee's best-loved movie, *Enter the Dragon*. The film introduced U.S. audiences to the wonder of martial arts and helped boost Jackie's career.

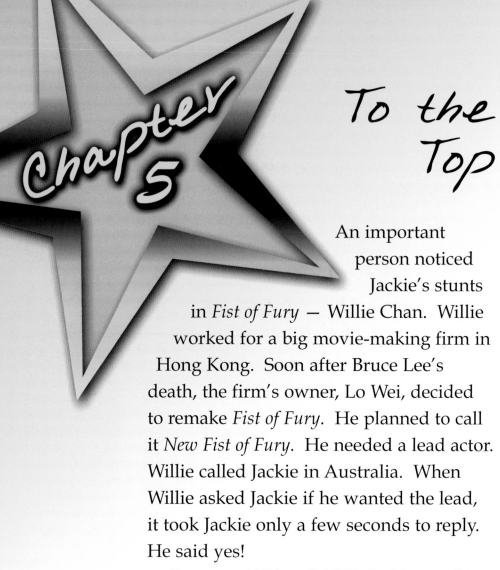

Chapter 5

To the Top

An important person noticed Jackie's stunts in *Fist of Fury* — Willie Chan. Willie worked for a big movie-making firm in Hong Kong. Soon after Bruce Lee's death, the firm's owner, Lo Wei, decided to remake *Fist of Fury*. He planned to call it *New Fist of Fury*. He needed a lead actor. Willie called Jackie in Australia. When Willie asked Jackie if he wanted the lead, it took Jackie only a few seconds to reply. He said yes!

Between 1976 and 1978, Jackie acted in nearly a dozen Hong-Kong-made martial arts films. Few of them did well at the box office. Jackie says that directors and producers made a mistake. They tried to get him and other martial artists to imitate Bruce Lee. Jackie refused. "No one wants to see a fake Bruce Lee," Jackie said.

Jackie has lived up to his "willing-to-try-any-stunt" reputation — but not without injuries. While jumping onto a hovercraft in *Rumble in the Bronx*, he broke his ankle. Doctors put a cast on it. They told him to rest. Jackie, however, had a movie to finish. He put a sock over his cast and painted a sneaker on top of the sock. Then he went back to work.

Finally, in 1978, Jackie starred in his first big hit, *Snake in the Eagle's Shadow*. The hugely successful *Drunken Master* came soon after. In both movies, Jackie broke martial arts and Bruce Lee traditions. "Bruce screamed when he hit someone to show his strength and anger. I say we should scream to show much hitting someone hurts your hand," Jackie wrote. "I think audiences want to see . . . someone who's not afraid to be a coward."

Adding Humor

Jackie also thought fans wanted to see humor. For example, when Jackie punches his enemy in *Snake in the Eagle's Shadow*, he yells, "I am a poisonous snake." Then he punches him in the stomach and screams,

"That's called finding the snake." The line made viewers laugh. We can thank Jackie for adding humor to the action-movie formula.

Except for a few flops, Jackie's movies — from the 1980s on — have done very well. Fans find his death-defying stunts thrilling. Plus, they enjoy his comedy. Some of the Hong Kong successes include *Winners and Sinners* (1983), *Project A* (1984), *My Lucky Stars* (1985), and *Armour of God* (1986). *Armour of God* became Hong Kong's third-highest grossing film of the 1980s. In 1994, *Drunken Master II* grossed more than U.S. $2.5 million.

Until the mid-1990s, Jackie's movies drew only a few American fans. *Rumble in the Bronx* changed all that. After opening in the U.S. in 1996, the movie made $10 million in its first week! Jackie's boyish good looks made him popular. His daredevil stunts made him a hero. Fans loved his willingness to lose a fight or two — before he beat his enemies.

Jackie admits that,

Fact File

Although Jackie has found great success as an action movie star, he is sad that he didn't learn more in school. He gives money to a charity that helps poor children go to school in China. The charity gives children books and clothing.

at first, fame and success went to his head. He says he became self-centered and not very nice to be around. In the late 1970s, he dated Teresa Teng Li-jun. She was a beautiful and popular singer from Taiwan. He admired her soft-spoken kindness and lovely manners. Jackie, however, showed almost no manners at all. When they dined at nice restaurants, he would treat the wait

In *The Legend of Drunken Master*, Jackie portrays the folk-hero and martial artist Wong Fei Hung as a young troublemaker (*below*). The film shows some of Jackie's finest fight scenes.

staff rudely. He even put his feet up on the table. "I loved her," Jackie writes, "but I loved myself more." Teresa soon grew tired of his poor manners and sent him on his way.

A few months later, Jackie met a successful actress from Taiwan, Lin Feng-jiao. She made him feel at ease. Jackie's manners improved. In 1982, after seeing each other for several years, he and Lin Feng-jiao married. Jackie says he is a lucky man because he found someone who loved him in spite of his faults. The couple has a son, Jaycee Chan. He is making a career for himself as an actor and a singer.

The more recent *Rush Hour* and the *Shanghai Noon* action-film series have increased Jackie's fame. His star appears in the Hollywood Walk of Fame. *New Police Story*, made in Hong Kong in 2004, earned him the Golden Rooster Award.

Jackie is generous with his money and his time. He donates millions of dollars a year to

Fact File

Tom Cruise is a big fan and a friend of Jackie Chan. Tom has donated $20,000 to Jackie's scholarship fund. This charity helps poor, talented students attend the Hong Kong Academy for Performing Arts.

Animated Chan

From 2000 to 2005, the Cartoon Network ran *The Jackie Chan Adventures*. In these cartoons, Jackie travels around the world with his niece Jade. They search for twelve charms that can protect the world from evil. Jackie and Jade use their martial arts to fight criminals also searching for the charms. For his role, Jackie won the 2002 Daytime Emmy Award for Outstanding Performer in an Animated Program. In September 2004, Sony released a PlayStation video game based on the cartoon.

Some of the animated *Jackie Chan Adventures* (*left*) mimic Jackie's movies. The episode *Tough Break*, for example, shows Jackie waterskiing with a cast on his leg. The bloopers at the end of *Rumble in the Bronx* show that Jackie wore a cast under his costume in that movie. He had broken his ankle during a stunt.

Jackie and Owen Wilson (*above*) costarred in *Shanghai Noon* and *Shanghai Knights*. Fans love these action-filled comedies — mainly because these two are so funny together. Jackie won this star in the Hollywood Walk of Fame in 2002.

such worthy causes as AIDS treatment and disaster relief. He sings at charity concerts. Jackie sees himself as a role model for children. He wants his movies to show action but not violence.

In 2006, Jackie announced that he and action-hero Jet Li plan to costar in a Hollywood movie. If they do, fans will see a lot of action. Jet Li is trained in the Chinese martial art of wushu. He can handle eighteen weapons better than anyone else. He won six Chinese national wushu contests in a row before he turned seventeen.

From his humble start, Jackie has gone far. He writes in his autobiography, "I was a useless child. A ragged boy. A reckless teen. And now — Look who I am now!" Jackie made the world watch him, and the world likes what it sees.

Time Line

1954	Jackie Chan is born in Hong Kong. His parents name him Chan Kong-sang.
1961	Jackie begins ten years of study at the China Drama Academy.
1971	Bruce Lee's hit movie, *Fist of Fury*, features Jackie Chan as a stuntman double.
1976	Willie Chan begins managing Jackie's career.
1978	Snake in the *Eagle's Shadow* and *Drunken Master* make Jackie a star in Asia.
1979	Jackie directs his first movie, *Fearless Hyena*. Asian audiences loved it.
1983	Taiwanese actress Lin Feng-Jiao and Jackie Chan marry. They have a son, Jaycee Chan.
1986	The making of *Armour of God* lands Jackie in the hospital. A blow to his head causes permanent hearing loss.
1994	*Rumble in the Bronx* is a big hit in the U.S.
2000	Jackie and Owen Wilson make *Shanghai Noon*, the first in a series of *Shanghai* movies.
2004	After the tsunami disaster, Jackie raises hundreds of thousands of dollars to help its victims.
2006	Jackie and Jet Li plan to make a Hollywood movie together.

Glossary

ambassador — someone who represents a nation or a cause and tries to promote it.

communists — people who believe that government — instead of individuals — should own all of a nation's resources.

cowers — hides or shrinks in fear.

creed — a set of beliefs or rules to live by.

emperors — supreme rulers who rise to power through inheritance rather than election.

endure — put up with, over time.

harnesses — straps or gears that hold or pull weight.

humble — modest or poor, not proud.

intercepting — stopping or hitting something out of the way before it reaches its target.

imitate — to act like someone else.

pulleys — small, fixed wheels with grooved rims in which a rope or chain runs.

stunt coordinator — the boss of stunt performers in a movie or play.

taut — pulled tight.

volunteered — offered to do something without being asked.

To Find Out More

Books

Bruce Lee. Greg Roensch (Rosen Pub. Group)

Day of the Dragon. Matt Christopher (Little, Brown)

Jet Li. Christy Marx (Rosen Pub. Group)

Kung Fu and Tai Chi. Ann Heinrichs (Child's World)

Martial Arts for Fun! Kevin Carter (Compass Point Books)

Sign of the Qin. L.G. Bass (Hyperion Books for Children)

Videos

Jackie Chan Adventures (Adelaide Productions) PG

Around the World in 80 Days (Buena Vista Pictures) PG

Web Sites

The Official Jackie Chan Web Site
www.jackiechan.com
Learn about Jackie's childhood in Hong Kong and his plans for new movies

Stuntman Career
library.thinkquest.org/3340/TOPSTU.HTM
Facts about the stunt performing – wages, working conditions, and training needed

Index

About the Author

An old fan of Jackie Chan, author Amy M. Stone wishes he would come to Milwaukee, Wisconsin, where she lives.

Amy has written ten nonfiction books for children. Her two children — now grown — have helped. They let her know if the rough drafts made sense and held their interest. They like her books about fascinating people, such as Jackie Chan. She hopes you will, too.